Count Each
Breath

Maria James-Thiaw

To Robin
Peace + Poetry
Maria James-Thiaw

Wild Ink Publishing
wild-ink-publishing.com

Wild Ink Publishing

A Wild Ink Publishing Original
Wild Ink Publishing
wild-ink-publishing.com

ISBN: 978-1-958531-03-7

"Oh, please. Those things come back negative for, like, seven years before they're positive."
~ my well-meaning orthopedic surgeon.

I dedicate this collection of poetry to all the enigmas: the women who suffer from invisible ailments that take years to diagnose.

I would also like to thank those medical professionals who listen to their patients, treat us as individuals, and take time to solve problems, even when we don't fit the textbook model.

Thank you to my family and close friends for their unending support of my art and my uniqueness. I love you all dearly.

Forward

    I complete this book in the minutes before the ball drops New Year's Eve, 2020. Tonight, New Year's Eve is different. There are no revelers in Time Square. Those that are out, don masked faces to protect others from sickness. My family and I stay in, peering through windows as the neighbors explode huge fireworks in their backyards.

    This is the year we've been beaten by the environment, the political climate, historic injustices, systematic inequities, and especially a deadly pandemic. I feel every blow we've collectively taken, but no matter how much time I have to breathe, I will breathe poetry into the world.

    This collection is one tick priming a tock on the face of this disastrous pandemic. It is a time capsule, telling the future who we were. Thank you for sharing this moment with me.

Table of Contents

I. Dispair-ities

II. Locked Down

III. Rise Up

Additional Works

1. Dispair-ities

Rage

The day
I thought I was dying
I decided

to carefully fold up my somedays,
keep them tucked in a trunk
in a cobweb-laced corner of a dark attic-
The kind of place where you
put things unfinished-
things that were never meant to be.

The day
I thought I was dying
I tried

to tug tightly closed divine doors open,
searched the web but couldn't see myself,
felt Dylan's judgmental gaze burned into my back.
I knew what he thought of weary me,
accepting fatigue, wrapped in that 'good night'
like a blanket, too afraid to rage.

The day
I thought I was dying
I chose

someone to haunt – not to scare,
someone to follow and leave
whispers like little gifts.
I'd be his cool breeze and his
'something told me.' The song
incessantly singing in his head.

The day
I thought I was dying
I searched

for a bucket to hold my 'will-dos.'
Tears formed and fell like wasted time,
clocks melted and slid off my cheeks,
streaming into shaky hands.
My mind flipped through mental pictures
of my boys, and the man who
 may not be Mother enough for them.

I raged.
I finally raged.
Firelight dances on the wick,
but never ceases to burn.

This is the Poem that Flashed Before My Eyes

When my hair stands up like crinkled screams of
silver independence from my intended black style,
will my voice be as wrinkled as my brow?

Aunties told me a change would come.
They gave cloudy warnings with fuzzy edges—
women, the keepers of secrets.
They didn't tell me babies could change
your shoe size till my pumps were at Goodwill.
This time, they drop hints in the fog.

My first poems were written inside me
as a fuzzy white bearskin rug tickled my cheek.
Eyes wide and ebony, I peered up at Daddy,
who seemed like a giant as he read aloud from
his long canary-colored legal pad.
My eyes thumbed through the stripes of
the brown plaid couch as I took up the gauntlet,
declaring within that my first written words
would have rhythm and rhyme.

I wrote those poems in purple crayon,
the color of God in a field,
as I tried to build my world the way Harold did.
White first graders couldn't pronounce
plagiarism, but they still accused me of it.
I, the cultural enigma, walked over a bed of hot
microaggressions each day.

Maria James-Thiaw

At puberty, my voice cracked open and
angst oozed out. Alone amongst the faceless,
I collected smart comments like coins on my tongue
hoping they'd pay my fare to the river's darker side.
Instead, Public Enemy walked me to school each day
I brought the noise with a giant clock around my neck.

Poems in my mouth, chapbooks on my back.
I came out of college a feminist with
enough rhythm in my big legs to make music.
The slam hustle, a game I played well before
TikTok, YouTube, Instagram.
Footwork carried my name to other venues.
I blessed mics from state to state in my twenties,
bounced craft from one brick wall to the next,
impressed players, sold CDs—
    Get the feature, get the feature, get the feature —
soaked the town in my song.
.

Energy wanes now, demands are heavy.
Poems turn grey. Young bucks know
your decade by the way you bless the mic.
What does the next one hold?
Will the poem of my life remain, or
will it wrinkle and melt away like time?

Nothing.

Nothing can be done,
she says as she flips a switch,
darkening the cloudy picture of
collapsing bones and narrowing discs.
She says she likes me for the way I
pull smiles from dark places.
All my doctors say that.

Nothing. Can. Be. Done.
How should I react?
Cast blame like a net into the sea?
Curse God? Pull at my hair? Weep?
I say nothing heavy, dark or daring.

Nothing. Can. Be. Done.
I'm well aware my bones refuse
to submit to my mind's music,
though my memories dance.

Nothing. Can. Be. Done.
I give the gift of spoken frivolities.
Jokes are wings for hearts
weighed down by truth.
She says she likes me.
I say,

Nothing can be
'done'
if you continue to smile.

Maria James-Thiaw

Chronic

I lay in bed stretching out old age like a fitted sheet.
It has blanketed me since my twenties.
At that age, doctors' ears free float away from you
as if they had wings attached.
Their eyes bubble, distort, then droop
like Dali's clocks as you point to hot, swollen joints.

Red means emergency. Red means stop.
Red is dull and unassuming on brown skin.

In the next room, a man with white hair holds a
melting muscle behind his crows' feet.
His joints are swollen too, distorting his fingers.
This does not need dissecting or figured out.
His keys are in the cookie jar; his watch is in the fridge.
His knees grind when he bends.

Red screams from pallid skin.
His ailments live in textbooks.

I limp to the mirror, each cautious step battles
the stiffness that has set in overnight.
Silver hairs fight black for domination.
They've planted themselves like a flag in foreign land.
They declare themselves sovereign and entitled to live here.
They tell me, because of them, my pain has meaning, but
I arrive in the office still black and thick as most of my mane.
He is blinded by the whiteness of his coat.

Red masks my vision as his eyes
bubble, distort and droop.
His face melts into the textbook again.

Chameleon

Who do I call when the color of dusk
spills from splotchy red fingertips into my palm?

Which doc covers digits that creak and diverge
different directions like death disturbed?

Will they handle broken lifelines, dry patches,
scratchy and white on my once brown parts?

What do I take when I can't remember them
as they were -- soft, stretchable, color of earth?

Thin wrinkles become red cracks,
ashen scrim stretched across inflamed veins.

Who are the heroes that extinguish this fire,
the phantom itch, the torture of pins in skin?

From mahogany to indigo, deep as jazz,
blue as Harlem tunes sinking into concrete,

blue as the look in a lost child's eyes, as
tears welling up in mine, then dismissed,

I ponder,
what type of doctor deals with this?

Hysteria

My immune system is on the blink.
Common colds collapse lungs,
hands shake, skin peels off in sheets.
My friend says hers hates melanin,
fights the skin she's in,
unpeels her like fresh fruit.

We share a smoker's cough
without the smoke,
this unnamed thief of words and air,
it shadows us on stage.
Stands in our spotlight.

My girl's babies cry for glory
on the courts, in the classroom, yet
her breasts respond like
they're still hungry bundles—
Now all her arms hold is the
lump and throb of her, a dripping faucet.

My friend's throat is a noose.
She becomes a caricature, eyes bulging.
Her sweat-drenched heart skips, runs
the way she hasn't since we were in school.

My sister's cells sickle like little warriors,
blinded, dowsing one another in friendly fire.
What a wonder, that woman whose cape
is art and sword is song.
She flies to fight injustice in the Motherland.
Forty is far too fresh for a heart to fail but fail it did.
She was 37.

Count Each Breath

But it was Rachel, the Trailblazer,
struck first in utero.
She had thunder bolts under her skin.
Pain laughed in the face of the morphine drip.
Hershey Med's biggest brains were
dim as a date night. Dumbfounded,
blinking replaced words—
the swoosh of eye lashes,
the creak of a furrowed brow,
the deep groove of questions scratched
into scalps— their silence, deafening.

I've got 7 syndromes, Rachel said, almost proudly,
like she'd beaten us at some game.
Seven complete syndromes and a cancer that
wrapped itself around her spinal cord like a little
girl on a gymnast bar.
My pregnant body wasn't offered a seat at
her standing-room-only funeral.

Am I the only one asking, why?
Why are sisters so sick?
Extraordinary sisters with
heavy, world-changing words,
innovative ideas, change-the-game dames,
with fibroids claiming wombs
coughs stealing voices,
sickling cells' mutinous immunity.

900 dollars monthly, fished from the pocket of
under-employed Rachel.
This is the cost of being descended
from slaves in the land of the free.

Black. Female. Fat. Stressed.
Diagnosis declared! You've got BFFS, a
dis-ease like conversion disorder or hysteria.

There's no cure.

Natural Woman

The ancients believed:
Name a thing, be empowered,
So, help me name this—

Skin-sheet peeling, breath-
stealing, crushing pain in chest,
tremors, joints inflamed—

Still, it has no name.
Like the bush burning, it is.
Heart skips, drags, and runs.

Names are powerful—
blood panel, biopsy, but
unidentified.

This is the nature
of woman. Neglected from
studies. Unnamed still.

She: A Haiku

There are shards in my
wounded womb. Vicious, slicing
up her safe place. She,

the little girl that
giggles, plays behind my eyes.
Her breathless whispers.

She was never born.
She was worth the pain. Alas,
why should I still try?

I can't usher her
into this world where she will
be used, discarded.

She-bodies belong
to everyone else. They are
never fully served.

Waiting Room

We clock watch waiting for words,
that won't fit comfortably on our tongues.
The sound, deafening, like the sight of
a guillotine quivering over one's head.

Our dreams paint pictures of worry,
our eyesight dwindles in blue lit biases
and misinformation, we wait for someone
to interpret language we may have
already encountered in pages
of dusty journals that wrinkle like skin.

We breathe deep to push away
the intense sense that our nightmares
got up and walked in with us.
That's when we notice
the essential oils wafting through the vents,
keeping the scent of death from
insulting our nostrils as
we clock-watch in the waiting room.

Voodoo Doll

My teeth free float in my mouth.
Held only by a thread of flesh,

they avoid the electric walls of my gums.
They are bells tolling.

If I could sleep, they would grind.
My eyelids are glued open.

My throat is sewn shut.
A witch sticks pins in my joints,

drills her thumbs into my hips,
pounds my head till my stomach churns.

They call this *mourning*.
I wake up in it.

Every day, I remind myself to breathe.
Not the quick, shallow breaths I feel,

but slow, steady, deep.
I tell myself I still want to.

True Patriot

I missed the fireworks this year.
Told the family to go ahead to the bridge
where the sky is clear.

Their excitement reflected in the rippling river.
Amidst neighbors, they gathered to watch
stars dance on a carpet of night in freedom's name.

I laid in bed alone. The house,
quiet but for my pounding heart, the
mini explosions, distant cheers.

I wore red, white and blue stars
to entertain and baffle white sheets.
They say activists can't be patriots,

but protest breathes life into the American dream,
and I come from a long line of revolutionaries,
the red, the brown, the black, the white,

whose fuel is the weighty knowledge
of our creed and the expectation
that we'd live up to it.

I drifted into dreaming, when suddenly,
eyes burst open, goblet tipped,
spilling a thick syrup of brown blood in me.

There was a suicide bomb in my womb.
My system, shell shocked, frozen in fear.
Brave heart drummed warnings— harder, louder.

Gauntlet down, my body, a true patriot,
prepared for the fight. Coats of white intervened,
then hours later, it earned its ticker tape parade.

Some of my neighbors on the bridge
are excited to peer over the rippling water
under a shower of light.

They see themselves in cowboy regalia,
in starred and striped clothes
as real, more real than us,

more real than I,
the inactive activist drowning in blood
under the color struck sky.

I say, love your country.
Love it broken, bleeding, infected,
and if your nation is sick,

raise your fist, take a knee,
drop a gauntlet.
Save it.

Day Seven

Bodies are music—
Systems in motion,
divine rhythm,
the dance of digestion,
the coronary flow.

Unending cycles
of reflection,
Creator, creation,
the meaning of
made in His image.

Maestro, the brain,
conducts a symphony,
writes a melody.
The heart's rhythm reflects
the Universe—

Womb cycles are moon cycles.
Photosynthesis is breath.
Tree rings grow in the lines of our palms.
Belly sounds are systems swirling
like dervishes in worship.

When one musician refuses to play
the rhythm is off.
No more leaps and spins
in time with creation.

Revelation—
my eyes open to old timers
who call sickness the devil—
the angel of music, forced out of the light.

He, like illness, is a
disruption of rhythm,
a clash of sounds,
a flat note,
an instrument out of tune,
distorted, a blur.

This ileus, then, is an
arrhythmia of Spirit
inciting the cries of stones.
The seventh day reveals
a direct attack on my song.

Prescription

Take one walk in the woods per day.
Breathe. Swallow the sounds of birds.
Let bare feet and grass make out
like wild-eyed teenagers.
Let your feet say yes. Let them kiss the grass back.

Breathe again.
Name each scent you ingest:
Flower.   Mammal.   Water.   Ghost.
Stop and squint toward the sound of lingering eyes.
Listen as they scamper away.

Breathe. Walk again as your mind sings.
Look for flowers the color of your song. Give thanks.
Bow to bugs that buzz by, offer them leaves to play with,
smile at a frog that greets you. Hop away.
Journey on till skinned knees call for kisses.

Arrive home before the moon rises to lead you there.

Under Glass

The sky is white under thick frosted glass.
My worries are small amidst tall trees that
dress their spines in white birch.
Piney branches balance heavy weights of snow,
They whisper,
> *Peace, let someone else carry it for now*

In this glass globe it is winter, without
pressure or deadlines.
It is a heavy snow, but not a storm.
Each flake slowly floats to the ground, painting
the scene clean.

The scent of pine tickles my nostrils
I breath in evergreens, exhale gratitude
as my mind takes sabbath
under this glass globe, tucked away
from the unclean world.

II. Locked Down

Essentials

One week before the shutdown, the gaping mouths of
empty store shelves set my eyes ablaze.
Items we normally have at our fingertips, elusive as dust.
Pandemic continues and I duck it by turning online.
Prices peak as panic sets in.
Don't call it rationing.
Too many memories, all of them bad.
Instead, signs cry, TWO PER CUSTOMER.
Hundreds of us need our share.
The grocery site can't deliver for five days.
The milk jug is empty.
Six feet apart, people snake around the grocery store lot
waiting for admittance.
The world is upside down. They said two weeks two months ago.
The nightmares are fierce. They walk during the day,
because we don't sleep.
I remember Grandma kept cash in her mattress,
cookie jar, underwear drawer.
I need a stash in case the market crash is permanent.
The bankers won't answer.
I am a red light flashing on their old push-button phone.
I pack plastic gloves and my last can of Lysol
to make my withdrawal.
I kiss my son goodbye and let the TV babysit him.
He is afraid to be outside.
Dozens of cars got to the bank first.
Dozens of hands pressed each key.
I spray down the ATM before I take out my cash.
I don't want to go home with anything
I didn't come here with.

Sheltered

Once two weeks roll into ten,
and case counts climb, doubling daily,
dreams turn into abstract paintings
of subconscious anxieties.

In daylight, your heartbeat skips as you
silently judge TV characters for touching,
for being mask-less on screen.

The kids call this Corona-cation.
They dismiss your references to
Max Headroom as the Zoom box
hugs your shoulders like a hostage taker.

It keeps you behind glass.
You've grown used to glitching,
your sk-sk-skipping tongue
like a needle on vinyl.
The kids disregard this too.

Meetings mount meetings and make more meetings.
Neither you nor your children can tell
if the work counts or if it just fills time.

Time is a dystopian misadventure.
The comedic masks the horrific tightly
so little inhalable bits of fear won't spew out.

Neighbor children stage protests in front yards,
rebelling against the values of grandparents
they haven't seen in weeks.

Count Each Breath

You hide in the backyard, rolling up joy
with shaky hands, polluting the air with
yellow clouds of pungent peace.

It makes the chalk-drawn rainbows
in the drive-way glisten.
The lynched teddy looks happy perched in your tree.

Your pet cocks his head sideways.
He wonders why you've been here so long.
Why don't you disappear each morning like you used to?

At six, peer out from your doors and windows and
welcome a nurse home with song and applause.
The Italians taught you this.

They make sense now. Tears pile at her feet like
tickertape. There. Now you've done something
honorable with your day.

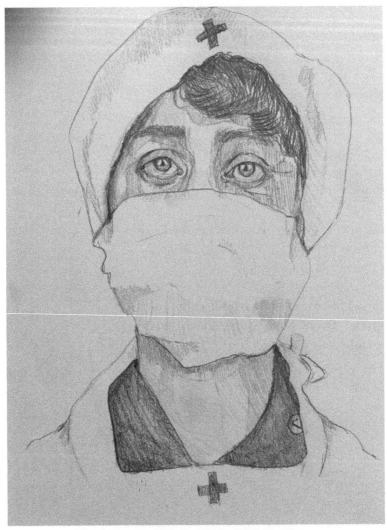

Drawing by Ruby Tilder, 11th grade.

"The fear of influenza is creating a panic, an unreasonable panic that will be promoted, we suspect, by the drastic commands of the authorities. ... Steer clear of it, therefore and talk of cheerful things – of health, for instance, instead of disease."

~ Philadelphia Inquirer, 1918

Spit Spreads Death

Her eyes scream.
The cross on her cap points toward Heaven.
The cross on her apron, close to her heart.
Dark bangs drop over brow as if from exhaustion.
Tight cloth masks nose and mouth.
It's caution tape,
a barrier between her and horror,
though all the while,
her eyes scream.

Piercing grey under heavy lids,
thin red tentacles reaching for iris
like claws—or did I imagine those?
There is something red about her
sepia expression, something
red and imposing in the colorless photo.

Her eyes scream.
They've seen death,
seen it coming in a wave
through reservations,
rural towns, workhouses,
seen it devour the poor,
seen it fill mass graves,
take whole families in a matter of hours.

Death has yet to touch her, but it's come close.
She's felt its hot, foul, sulfur breath on her neck.
It came here with the parade
politicians planned to fund their war.
When science and politics mix,
politics win and this city where the
constitution was signed was too proud,
too American to shelter in place.

Her eyes screamed when she saw them
gathered there, shoulder to shoulder,
ungloved hands waving flags. Unmasked
cheers flying from mouths.
Instruments spitting out anthems.

They hadn't listened,
Hadn't seen it,
Hadn't felt its sulfur breath,
but they would. They would.
In a few days they would.

She prepared beds for them
inside stretched hospital walls,
hotels, parishes, colleges.
Death came for them with arms wide,
with reinforcements to flatten the morgue
with their bodies - 12,000 souls lost.

Her eyes scream
above the cloth tight enough to block
death from her mouth, so she hopes.
The striking black caption, visible on walls,
trolley cars, and lampposts says it all:

Spit Spreads Death
She knows it's so.

Her eyes scream.

The 1st Fourteen

I.

Friday the 13th, the alarm sounds
We're all sent home.
Monday, the kids will become

tiny squares or voices without faces
or shells of themselves
or milk carton pics.

You've seen a kid without a grin.
Have you seen a grin without a kid?
We're all mad here, wondering

when does conversation turn deadly?
Can the plague march through band class
from sax to trumpet to trombone?

Can it dance in the Spring musical?
Can it sit in the orchestra seats?
In the balcony?

Can it learn poetry,
write eulogies for the Before Times?
For our grandparents?

My God, what about our grandparents?
How hard do we stretch to be six feet apart?
If a mask is enough to save us, then why,

America, Land of Plenty,
were you caught without enough?

II.

The economy's switch has been flipped to *off*.
Stores crowded, shelves empty.
They say the virus can live on boxes.
For no extra fee, they'll deliver it to your house.

My creative brain scurries into the dark,
curls in on itself in the back corner of my head.

III.

I've got no words.

No, you can't play outside.
No, your friends can't come over.
No, you can't have a birthday.
No, more summer camp this year.
No, we can't see Grandma.
No, you can't see Pop Pop.
No, we can't spend the money.
No, I can't watch the news.
No, don't touch that railing.
No, don't touch that fountain.
No, don't touch that friend.
Don't touch that railing, that fountain, that friend!
No, don't touch the box till I spray!
No, I don't know when daddy's coming home.
No, the embassy isn't answering.
No, the senator isn't answering.
No, the airport is not answering.
I don't know when daddy is coming home.
No, daddy's not dead.
No, daddy's not dead.
No, daddy's NOT dead.
For Christ sakes I'd tell you if daddy was dead!
No, I'm not okay. Of course, I'm not okay. Hell no, I'm not okay!
But it's okay. No one else is either.

We are writing to inform you that your
husband has been fired for job abandonment.

What?!
No. Daddy's not dead.
No. Words.

IV.

Mother Africa ties up her borders
to block the disease.
You get tied under her mask,
 accused of job abandonment.

I tuck money into dresser drawers
the way Great-Aunt Lois
balled up dollars in her bra.

I remember the photos of breadlines –
black men elbow to elbow in the shadow
of a billboard promoting America dreaming.
How will they socially distance a breadline?

I turn on the news. I find out.

V.

The psychics are still employed.
The theaters are empty.
My actor-waiter friend reads tarot on social media.

Tell me again what the Death Card means.

VI. Rebirth

Seven days shut in,
catharsis brings renaissance.
My poem-bone heals.

VII.

Day seven,
a Margaret Attwood documentary
unlocks small spurts of
constipated verse with talk
of dystopia, dictatorships, and handmaids.

Blessed be. It's happening.

VIII.

Day 8: Write. Read. Repeat. In cyberspace, poets find safe places to meet. The Orwellian hoards will come for us first, we know, but gathering and sharing brings peace. We reminisce, weave brain pictures of nights sculpting images in the museum, on the street, in the bar, on the page. We laugh as we share, and the muse creeps back into us. We are a magician's top hat. Hand over hand, one by one, she pulls the hidden words out.

IX.

Another documentary: *The Spanish flu.*
A year before my grandmother's birth,
it happened.

The experts called for social distancing.
The politicians put profits over people.
The people cried, *Freedom!* They had a parade
big enough to showcase the American ego.

Days later, the stench of their bodies filled
clogged city streets. 40 million.
Nurses made signs: *Spit Spreads Death.*

I post this everywhere.

X. Sensing Shadows

I've seen shadows before,
those that dart just out of view
avoiding gaze and question, others
looming, threatening, pressing their thoughts
into yours by force until you feel the foul
sound of their voices.

The shadows I see now hide,
peek around corners, warn,
introduce themselves, demand attention,
or run from it.

Once the pandemic threw us upside down
the shadows became small, darting
here to there, slithering out of sight,
sneaking into my view then ducking away again,
like an infestation in its early stage—
something is coming.

These little ones are a message:
*You are just beginning. The bell has not
tolled on this plague.*
I just pray, when the smoke clears and we
emerge from the prison of our own homes, that
I will be more flesh than shadow.

XI. School

Quarantine is a sadistic medieval henchman.
I meet my students online and assign this—
    Document the moment with poetry.
My young geniuses offer Suess-style rhyme,
or blood red microphones.

    Ausome-Alex submits a cynical lyric called:
    I Hate Poetry.
    Bebe sits catatonic in her window seat.
    C.J.'s mom yells in Arabic as her puke stains the rug.

Kids' minds are on the rack, their potential
bleeding and stretched.
I can relate.

I turn to my own sons, one furiously typing
red, all-caps, death threats to his teacher,
the other, sobbing, back turned to his webcam.

I am still.
My eyes under heavy lids at our home-made kitchen-table-school
just wait for the bell to ring.

XII.

If I leave the house, I'll need a mask.
I refuse to leave the house.
My student doesn't leave her room.
My son puts a handkerchief over his head
and holds his breath on the front porch.
He can't go any farther than that.

XIII.

Quietly, rage bubbles up inside
the way water rises in a deep dug
desert hole, a surprise to the digger.
My rage doesn't stomp or kick.
It just makes bad choices—

Smoke for cystic lungs,
fat and sugar tucked into belly folds,
wine for a mind twisted with worry.

Africa holds on. America's borders, closed.
I face the apocalypse alone as
the dead become numbers.
1,000 left the world last night,
with no one to see them off,
loved ones afraid to share their air.

I can't get air.

XIV.

It was supposed to be over by now.
Hope dresses in dark cloth
while we wonder what,
in the name of God,
could the rest of the month hold?

Point of View

My beloved has never
mastered the workings of
the female mind, only
tried to solve the unsolvable.
Too much dogma tattooed on
the backs of his eyelids,
scrawled on the walls of his veins.
He can't forgive frailty. Forgiveness is
an art practiced by Spirits, not men.

Moon rises.
The apocalypse steals our sleep,
but he picks up his anxiety, balls it like
putty between palms, throws it behind a veil.
God is good, he says, locking it into place,
God is good.
All the time, I reply, though my putty is stretched,
dripping like slime from my hands,
embedded in my hair, tangled, immovable.

Is it the tight cotton mask, or the news of the dead
that grips my throat and has the thin air
spiral around me when I'm in a store?
I blast music to drown sounds out, but
horsemen's hooves are hard to ignore.
I can hear my vertebrae grind when my head
turns to see what strangers stand too close.
The throbbing tone in my ears vibrates
like the heavy drag and gong of a bell that tolls.

My beloved says dystopia
shouldn't make fear walk in the world,
shouldn't make you sicker than the sickness.
He says I'm spoiled by freedom,
too sheltered to combat an apocalypse alone.
'Frailty, thy name is woman,'
I think he thinks as he reminds me: *God is good.*
All the time, I reply, though I feel the land
is littered with mines—

The fact is, wasn't it God that sent the Horsemen
in the first place?

Long Night

When the house is quiet, but for the
rhythmic breaths of little kings in their beds,
my heaviest thoughts try to tiptoe through the dark.
The floorboards creak under their feet.
They assault my mind, steal my rest.
The back and forth grooves my shape into the mattress.
Sleep lost, memories arise, quiet thoughts
raise their voices, corrupting me in the night. They say—

One died from cancer at the age of 51.
  One died at 28 from sitting too long,
    One died at 35 after he called all his peeps,
  One died at 19 on an ice coated street,
 One died when the landlord finally snapped,
One died when police were on the attack,
  One died when weak legs sent him tumbling downstairs,
  One died, heart and brain had a tear.
    One died in front of his kids, by his own desperate hand,
    300,000 died this year on the whim of a madman.

And everyone says, *God is good,*
but the weeping endures, the night is long,
and even the most devout, might not make it to morning.

Funerals

At Eddie's funeral his buddy told a joke
that no one understood. A joke for himself, and
the deceased. An inside joke, birthed in his
mind, planted in the open, baby-blue casket.

The church was silent, but for the sounds of
sniffles, and a child's imitation of Wile E. Coyote
as if his Acme anvil was the joke falling flat, but I
felt another sound. I felt Eddie's laughter bubble up
in my chest. I closed my eyes and there he was,
chuckling, that smile beaming. There was his,
Man, you crazy! and I couldn't help but attract the
stern eyes of white-gloved church mothers as
I laughed out loud.

The grace of gathering our goodbyes
together at the end of a life, pouring them
out with prayer and song, feeling the energy
of family and friends in proximity, gathered
for a common purpose, sharing the same
feeling as if our hearts had hands to hold--
that is a balm for the broken.
That is medicine.

At the end of Eddie's service, his wife
draped in black, came to hug me. Her
embrace felt like falling, falling, falling too
fast, too low, frightening – I didn't mean
to push her away, but I couldn't get lost in
there, too.
Sometimes empathy is warm and electric.
Sometimes empathy has fangs.

Count Each Breath

Pandemic funerals are streamed online.
A body in a room with only a few masked faces.
Most of us pay our respects in pajama pants,
leaned on kitchen counters drinking coffee,
lying in bed, or sitting at kitchen tables, distracted
by hungry pets or quarreling kids.

The spirit lays quiet these days, their caskets closed.
They died alone to avoid infecting others.
They died with a tube down their throat.
They died too fast to confess, or wish, or bless, and
there's no one there that can plant a joke or feel them
laugh.

But one thing remains. It's those fangs, sunk deep into
flesh and spirit, tearing us up inside and
we're all falling, falling, falling too fast, too low,
frightened and there's no one to hold on to
or push away and there's no way to know how long
we will be lost in here.

Community

The white supremacist out my window
is taking a break from harassing today.
He won't stare at my children,
or run to the nearest sympathizer
to share his poison about us.
He isn't shaking his fist in my direction,
or throwing me that practiced skinhead glare.

According to his page, today's focus is
our common enemy – chronic pain!
Clearly, this could be a crumb,
a way to steer 105 of my wokest-woke white friends
off the scent of his racist rants,
a way to confuse the social media police
with their "community standards,"
a way to keep black acronyms off his doorstep.

Today, on Juneteenth, in the middle of a revolution
BLM aren't terrorists or racists for him.
Today, the message is plain:
The white boy's in pain,
and I get it.

Yesterday, rainbowed words appeared
to grow like wildflowers out of my grass
despite his presence.
> *In this house, we believe*
> *Kindness is first,*
> *Black Lives Matter,*
> *Love is Love…*

Count Each Breath

and there he stood, flared up like a firework in July,
the clenched fists, the redness rising from chin up over
the skin of his exposed scalp.
Oh, how it churned in his belly
when someone shared his post with me,
that loudmouth black racist with her BLM sign...

He soon learned how loud a mouth could get,
as I chucked my own piercing words across the street.
He was crippled under the anvils of my voice, as it
thrust its discontent into his yard, with a hearty, full-caps curse.
Then, two by two, all day long, anti-racists planted themselves
in my front yard, their eyes directed toward his.

The white supremacist out my window
Attacked online on Juneteenth, despite
a revolution and got so worked up that
his nerves burn like crosses on each vertebrae.
Today his gnarled joints can't even
lift a finger to post a mean meme.

Rest well, nemesis. Wrap up in an old
red, white, and blue blanket of privilege,
or maybe your granddad's white robe.
At least doctors believe your pain.
You're not a drug seeker or thick-skinned or
stronger somehow.
Maybe they'll even give you something for the
the migraines you got from the blinding glow
of Beloved Community that sat in unity
on the other side of the street.

Covid Hair:
If Pigeon Peas Could Speak

My undercut is a God-given garden
where pigeon peas grow by the hundreds-
Tiny, round, wake-the-princess peas
cultivated by Covid lockdowns. Explore the growth.
They massage your skin.
Fingertips drawn in deep.
So deep hands think they've sunk into a cloud.
My pigeon peas are divine.
Pray with them like rosary beads.
Feel what they reveal. Listen close.
Hear them speak:

> We came here with Eve.
> She gave us to Abel and Cain.
> We kept the sun from burning
> Adam's neck as he walked along the Euphrates.
> We are Mesopotamia and Cush.
> We know the Tigris and the Nile.
> We laid in a basket made of reeds and
> We were pushed down river on the head of the chosen one.
>
> The angel commissioned to count us,
> coiled each one of us along the way,
> making nature's only perfect circle, and spread us
> throughout the diaspora like light spreads through darkness.
> We are in Ethiopia with the Holy Grail.
> We are in Timbuktu hiding ancient scrolls.
> We are Noah: We survived the flood.
> We're the shield that frees you to dance under the equatorial sun,
> and we are so faithful, so infinite, so tough,
> we return stronger with every rain.

"To be a Negro in this country and to be relatively conscious is to be in a rage almost all of the time."

~ James Baldwin

III. Rise Up

Terra Rocks

Terra rocks, moans, sheds breath heavy as her belly
battered by birth pains. Her *hee hee whoooo*
brings no relief from contractions,
four centuries apart, getting closer.
The squeeze steals resolve, rests, erupts again.
It comes in waves, the tearing tsunami of pain—

Super spreaders in carona-colored hats,
dark faces threaten blue, just by existing,
Karen "Amy Coopers" a stranger.
He is shot before her latte cools.
Boogaloo bullies paint peaceful protesters into corners.
Distract, destroy, dilute the message. They
call them terrorists for repeating his last words:
   I. Can't.
hee hee whoooo, hee hee whoooo.
The pains return.
Breathe, Terra, breathe.

Down low, Mother Earth dilates like flesh.
Like water, the bough breaks.
Critical thinkers hear the cry--
   Stay home. Protect one another.
Children hang rainbows in windows again,
tie teddy bears to trees, as
wine glasses sing us to sleep.
We hobby, we bake, some are
long haulers, some even survive,

but I, one of the vulnerable ones,
cradle my breath in African cloth,
so my face can protest from a distance
with my mouth safely closed.

Mobilizing

These days I need
accommodations to
get in trouble—
good trouble.
Necessary trouble.
A scooter with a hot pink
cushion, so while seated,
I can stand for women.
Red, black, and green
wrapped arms, a resting
place for clenched fists
with a slot for a picket,
tightened like truth, so
my sign won't lean,
planks of purple to
gird up swollen feet
and a motor that
buzzes songs
of solidarity and
freedom. I shall
overcome, I shall
overcome, because
in my scooter I can
get in trouble –
good trouble.
Necessary trouble.
In my scooter,
I am unstoppable.

A Sista's Elegy

If I were to die in 2020,
don't say you didn't pray right.
Don't say God wasn't good.
Don't say doctors didn't doctor
or that science was too slow.

If I were to die in 2020,
don't blame ancestry, aerosols, appetite,
blood that sickles, blood like sludge,
cravings overtaking, or cancer's claws on organs.

If I were to die in 2020,
don't blame schools for schooling,
my love of teaching, or
kids who can't envision
mortality and mask.

If I were to die in 2020,
it's not a pastor that didn't pastor enough,
a friend that wasn't friend enough,
a bond that wasn't tight enough.

If I were to die in 2020,
decorate the hearse like a wedding car—
tie cans to back bumper,
balloons and BLM flags flying.
Shoot, hashtag, and share
pics and this poem.

Let jazz lead my ravaged body through
frustrated streets where the echoes of
activist chants still bounce off stone walls.
Let white window chalk stir the sleeping
with its scream.

Jet-draw it with smoke across sky:

> *Here lies another world-changing woman*
> *gone too soon.*
> *Her words were sacrifice breathing,*
> *still beating in the chests of students she touched.*
> *When you wake, you'll see the God in her*
> *was the God in you, is the God in us.*

And if 2020 were to end with me
lying in repose in shadows of ivory,
may I still be a tool to tear down evil systems.
For the only ones to carry the blame,
if I were to die in 2020,
are the ones who slept through it all.

In Loving Memory of Kim Saunders, & Pastor Retha Tucker

Dueling Shadows

Daddy remembers the night he saw them,
amidst sweet fallen pecans and rows of
bright, downy clouds of unpicked cotton.
Those acres, purchased and farmed by freedmen
in a state that still owned slaves, was
passed down the ladder of time.

The field hugs one side of Hall Road,
while the cemetery and the church
great great-grand father Adam built,
sit on the other side.
Rising from rich, red soil full of music,
yasssuhs, amens, and soul –swelling
Mmmmmhmmms.

My daddy, at 4 years old, saw them,
the shadow-men that roam the field,
in this red resting ground for my ancestors,
this soil watered by the shout, stomp,
and sweat of black people.

There were two of them, looking like man-shaped
empty spaces in the dark. Only one fought for my daddy,
a 4-year-old boy who clutched his
grandma, Bama, in fire light
as a mob of white-robed men erected their
wooden manifesto in front
of their home.

The night he saw them,
he felt the cold sting of spirits,
smelled the smoldering hellfire,
heard the bickering back and forth,
words swinging to and fro, growing sharp as a knife's edge.

Not the warm-blooded devils
under white robes, but the
shadow men in the field arguing,
as the crowd sang southern gospel,
as the crowd swung rope over tree limb,
as the crowd pulled that rope.
He saw the shadow men roll dice,
cast bets on his future.

Opening the Gates

"And, anon, there strikes the ebony clock which stands in the hall of velvet.
And then, for a moment, all is still, and all is silent save the voice of the clock.
The dreams are stiff-frozen as they stand."
--Masque of the Red Death, Edgar Allen Poe

The ebony clock tick tocks to
the rhythm of my great granddaddy's
feet as he still saunters, high-headed,
down Hall Road in Georgia.

Only the gifted can see him now,
when he slips into the rhythm of his past life
and winks at honey-toned ladies leaving church,
imagining the red heat rising in their cheeks,
a twinkle in their mahogany eyes,
or when the night rolls in, and
he lurks in trenches along
the roads' edge, armed, ready,
imagining his neighbors beside him
waiting for the Klan to ride by.

His memories replay as dead memories do
when specters hang around long after
the clock has chimed—
that time-halting musical signal of the end.
Now the ebony clock tick tocks to and fro
to the rhythm of his feet and
he peers deep into the light he's been avoiding.
He sees folk getting ready. Folk making room.
A revelry in the heavens, iron gates unchained,

They about to open up.
Ain't been preparations like this since
the world was at war, he thinks.

An influx is coming.

My great granddaddy waits in the trench
he dug 10 decades ago knowing the
ebony clock's tick tock will stop it's dull,
heavy, monotonous clang
and release a chime from its brazen lungs.
All will be still then, as a parade of Georgians
march toward glory.

If he sees one of his kin on their way to the light
he'll take their hand and tell them,
> *I didn't want to leave the red clay. Couldn't*
> *stand to say goodbye,*
> *just mumbled a lie and jumped the train,*
> *taking my last look at Georgia.*
> *The Klan done run me out for shooting them off they*
> *horses. I ain't know they was police and politicians*
> *under them robes. The hateful. The heartless.*
> *Men with power to break up families,*
> *treatin' black lives like trash.*

He would take their hand and make them
understand, *I had to go North. Had to shelter in*
place to protect y'all from the plague of hate back home.

He quarantined in Detroit, planning to return when
things had changed, when the demons were
unmasked, and the pathogen of racism stopped
spreading in the land of his birth, but he died alone
of pneumonia in the palm of a neglectful healthcare
system. He returned as a specter waiting for his
shame to let him cross over.

Count Each Breath

But how could great grands understand my world, he thought--
a world where Negro lives meant nothing,
where healthcare was unequal,
where politicians lie to protect profits over people?
They can't forgive me, he figured, they can't understand.

The ebony clock tick tocks to and fro to the rhythm
of my great granddaddy's feet
as he walks away from the light once again,
head hung low.
He hunkers down, stiff-frozen as a dream deferred
in the trench he dug decades past
alongside Hall Road in Georgia.

Maria James-Thiaw

Burning Question: A Flashback

He was as Irish and as Catholic as his red hair
and freckles could assume. The black dots in
the center of his piercing blue eyes zeroed in
on me, their reflection.

I sat stifled by them, a tight wooden desk, a plaid
skirt, and a Peter Pan collar.
His question gripped my throat and squeezed-

Why are black people burning LA?

As if my mother hadn't dropped me off that
morning in her rocker paneled Volvo
at his over-priced school.

As if I were forty, not fourteen, and
held a terminal degree
in poverty, injustice, and Fannie-Lou-Hamer-tired.
As if I were not an infinitesimal dot in his otherwise
achromatic school's social circle.

That morning, he deemed me both authority and culprit of
indefensible acts against the glory of Hollywood.
Uncivilized, violent, dangerous, rage misplaced.

And me, in my youth and my privilege, though darker than
his own, sat wordless and weak
under the weight of his ignorance, boxed in and
labeled by his miseducation, until I spun
the heads of sisters in ear shot. I shook the
crucifixes with my answer:

"Fuck should I know, white boy?"

Count Each Breath

I sat a little taller then, satisfied that
after detention, in solidarity,
I would sit in suburban safety and sing
"We Don't Need no Water"
while watching the evening news.

My Pulmonologist

My pulmonologist is a woke chick
slim as the stick I'm measured against.
Pretty smile and bright eyes may blind
the big brains but she has the education
and fact remains,
my pulmonologist is a woke chick.

A scientist
elbow deep in the lungs' anatomy,
she understands the holes inside me, while
antibodies make the "whys" a mystery.
Never fat shaming or color blind,
she has time to text back or drop a line.

She sees the white coats put my pain in quotes.
When they can't see me, they change my name:
OBESE – all caps and underlined.
Enigma – mystery, unsolved.
Anxiety – all in my head.
Ignored – overlooked again.
My pulmonologist is a woke chick

Stress is the choke hold making
tricky airways restrict, so
when I say *I can't breathe she knows*
It's not just the lung collapse,
the inflammation or the scarring.
It's bigger than the blebs or blood.
She knows I hurt like a mama hurts,
and grasping that is a start to
seeing where this sickness comes from.

Count Each Breath

My pulmonologist is a woke chick.
Though wrapped up in PDE and pandemic,
she intubates the city streets with her feet
marching with millions screaming "I can't breathe!"
Fighting a revolution with me,
her voice is a tourniquet around blocks soaked
in black men's blood.
While illness keeps me home,
she's an ally with love, so, I say,
my pulmonologist is a woke chick.

Dedicated with gratitude to Dr. Caitlin Clancy, Harron Lung Center,
Penn Medicine, Philadelphia

Karen

The Karen, in her
natural habitat is
queen of her castle.

Her pedestal shakes.
Her fragility, her rage,
her murderous scream.

Common Thread

I guess his affiliations
with the same prejudice
he uses to guess mine.

His arms and feet crossed
like the stripes on his
red, plaid flannel shirt.
Jeans, too blue, too straight,
hair slightly whiter than his aged skin.

He glares when we giggle,
as if capturing our eyes
could control, quiet us.
Our heavy joy drags down
the edges of his mouth further,
further till it looks like an umbrella
on his grey-cloud face.

Privileged

My breath weighs the same as hers.
I hold it, the way she holds her handbag
closer as we pass by.
A raised fist is a lit fire in her mind.

My rage is real and dirty. It
clogs the air like smoke,
wraps around her throat—
she can't breathe.

But my sons know,
fear fueled by fallacy hurts more.
It blinds the eyes,
twists toys into weapons,
boys into beasts.
Nothing does damage like
a flame that can never cease to burn.

Contusion

America swells black and blue.
Not melting pot or tossed salad.
Shackled. Slave ships.
Black and blue lives in cities down.
"Blue Matters is fact. Black, a reminder."

Black. Blue. America down.
Words have lives too.
We need more than hashtags,
more than thoughts and prayers.
No more trolling internet-muscled
minions, no more naïve well-wishers
with their claims of color blindness.
It takes privilege to close one's eyes,
to reduce the world to black and white.

There is no radical war wish, no
homogeneous hoard of hate.
We march, fists and voices to the sky, to
dismantle systems that pit
black and blue against each other.
We stand... too many of us fall.

We weep in black, deluded white.
We go out to prove we won't be stopped.
Won't lock ourselves in.
They'll do that for us.
Dae'Anna in the back seat stays locked in
place, the place of trauma and blood.

Like the hair that needs cut and the pants
that need pulled up and the too dark eyes
and the nose too wide.
Like the yes sir, no sir,

look down,
look up,
hands up,
hands cuffed,
don't shoot!
Please sir, no thank you
My neck, my neck
I can't breathe.

We're licensed to carry a deep
down guttural pain like mama's wail,
the steel grip around empty bellies.
We can't inhale peace in any form.
Fists high, we cry for justice that never comes.

We pave the streets with the power
of tears, march as fear paints
targets on our backs—
Emmett, Tamir. George, Trayvon,
Philando, Sandra, Breonna, Sean

For over 1200 gone in the last five years.
We rise on the shoulders of ancestors,
unshackle our hope, and march again.

A collaboration with Marilyn Kallet

A Fuse Blew

A fuse blew the night we found out.
It was right before the rains came,
beating on the glass panes like fists,
like heads on concrete.

A fuse blew the night we found out, so,
we sat in the dark, hot expanse of a
warehouse behind a coffeehouse.
Espresso and art energized the stage.

Sankofa was purple from passion and pain.
Dustin took us there all night and all day.
The Priestess struck us like lightning.
Soul Cry made you want to taste the rainbow.

The unlit stage hooded Tiger's face,
for no one can see a black boy in the
dark when the rains come.
No one can see a black boy
in the dark when the rains come,

and the night was as heavy and thick as
Shane's poems are true.
Indeed, we heard it then from lips that
had just spit the deepest wisdom,
a Ghetto Issued proclamation.
GI was a herald to we, the scribes, and
we almost clapped out of habit, we almost
snapped out of habit—
    we almost snapped out,

because we had heard it then.
Smartphones buzzed like black women
on the back pew. We shared a

gasp, exchanged curses, questioned the verdict.

George Zimmerman: NOT guilty!

NOT GUILTY?!!!

A fuse blew.

Double-Sided

If they can't see it bleeding
they say it doesn't hurt. If they
can't hear the screaming,
they pretend we're not in pain.

Gloved finger to pursed lips says:

Shhh. Go slow.

We are a tree falling alone in the forest.
You shield your nose as we decay.
You fear ours, wide set. We are your they and them
with those rap songs, and dashikis and black fists.
We are your tremble and your tight throat.
We are you sweating under parasols of guilt.
We are the heat of accusation.

You, with your Jesus said, and All lives Matter,
licking grease from Chick-fil-a fingers,
you're our they and them—

The *I don't' see color* them,
My *family didn't own slaves* them
*Cops have a tough job to d*o them
What about Chicago them
They don't respect authority them
They can't block traffic them
Outside agitators them

Them, them, them, them,
muzzling my pain before they're bitten, them.

You say you mean well. You think that is enough.

Tortured Mind

The pandemic ties minds to the rack,
breaks brains like backs on the Catherine wheel.

My autistic child threatens self-harm—
and his teacher. And his brother.

A terroristic demand all caps and underlined, bold and red
as if the words 'die painfully' weren't enough.

In the ER, a patient calls us 'niggers.' Police surrounded him
as if their badge were a force field between my fingernails and his face.

Does mental illness excuse him, in this white room,
from stoning us with his forefather's words?

What is my excuse? I am the only one that can hear the cries
of my ancestors. No one sees me choke on their tears.

Eventually, the doctor says a hospital stay would be nothing
but a scold's bridle to quiet my son as he continues to hurt.

They send us home with a paper that tells him to breathe,
to call on his mother for help.

My mind turns to George Floyd crushed by a wall of blue.
I see my son. I hear that patient calling me out by name.

 I see the blue wall between us and feel the heavy white
concrete blocks of the hospital room repeatedly hit our heads.

Life Matters

First, Treyvon. A rainbow in
his pocket, a hood on his
head. Smashed into concrete
like little more than a bug. Shot dead on a snack run.

That first awakened the deep black fear, that
griping cramp that hurts so far down you know
your ancestors feel it too.

Then Michael,
left laid out, lifeless,
the amalgamation of blood and earth
painted a picture of black crimson rage.
Then Freddy in Mobtown, fires clawed
through concrete for life snuffed out.

Then, Eric, who they climbed like a mountain.
White arm locked like a bear claw around his
throat, squeezing, squeezing, squeezing till
blue lips spit out words, small. Final:
I. Can't. Breathe.

Then, a new tool, Facebook Live shows
Officer Shaky Hands killing Castille in his car.
Next day, Alton Sterling is dead.
Lurking emojis turn red.

Then, signs signal danger-
Educated Black Woman,
Sandra Bland, on route to university. Her
mind, sharp as a weapon. Her tongue, a
wick that could not be extinguished—
not without a noose.

Then, George's dead mama came to meet him
as the blue knees lynched him for nearly nine
minutes.

He pushed out those three familiar words,
three earth shaking, world changing words:
I. Can't. Breathe.

Millions mask up and put feet to pavement
but still, the karens call.

Help! Black man walking. Walking?
Walking through the blackest of nights,
Elijah seemed "suspicious." Deemed dangerous.
His mask was a hug that helped him face the world.
Another snack run with a tragic end.

Then, so many more, hung like rocks
'round our necks in blue ocean.
Our breath borrowed, like time.
We woke, wary of the very air.
I'm just different, Elijah pleaded.
I'm just different, that's all!

When your child's needs are special,
it gets heavier. Pulls you lower. Each story
adds weight to the knee on your neck.

Now Miami,
23-year-old sits wide open playing
with noncompliance.
His mental health worker, black,
lay bleeding beside him, hands up.

Don't. Shoot.

Count Each Breath

And the cop said he didn't mean to fire at the
caretaker, didn't mean to steal our breath
again, didn't want to be another blue
headline.

He was aiming for the other one—

nonverbal, misunderstood,
toy truck in hand.
I'm just different. I'm different, that's all.

When your child's needs are special,
the weight gets heavier, but
their lives matter, too.

The Great Awokening

Don't hand me
the burden of your
apology. The personal
isn't equipped to
address the systematic.

Don't crush my head with words that make
it hard for you to stand.

When George cried out,
        "Mama!" he
was my son.

When George said,
        "I can't breathe," I
felt breath forced from
        my lungs.

When they dismissed his cries,
I was tossed aside.

So, my back is too bent,
my hands too small
to carry the scales
that have finally
fallen from your eyes.

#Activism

Status updates are signs.
We angry emoji our opposition,
share pink pussyhat pics,
imagine joining the thunderclap of
feet to pavement. We stream.
We shake the world.

Radicalized

There's a glow in the window of the house across the street
where a troll has opened himself to the pull of algorithms.

They latch on to him the way demons whisper
to kids with their souls open.

They feed him what he is hungry for—
someone to blame.

They could have led him anywhere –
Isis, Black Israelites, Russian propoganda

but he was raised on the blue soil of Appalachia where guns
and religion determined your patriotism,

and empty pockets leave a bitter taste on the tongue.
Who will pay? Everyone.

The algorithms' milk is sweetened by fear.
He suckles all day.

In the dark, the finger pointed my way
looks blue as dissent,

he trashes liberals on the mayor's page,
shares sensational headlines.

The algorithm urges other trolls to applaud him, and they do. They're
rewarded with a platter, served up by QANON conspiracists,

stuffed like prizes in cereal boxes, with calls for war and
DIY bomb building videos.

Count Each Breath

There's a white glow in the window of the house across the street,
the whir of machines,

the steady hum of mumbled mad ranting, and
a shaky finger,

colored by the azure glow of the algorithm,
points in my direction.

Additional Works by Maria James-Thiaw:

Poetry Collections:

Windows to the Soul,
Shippensburg University Press

Rising Waters,
Shippensburg University Press

Talking "White,"
postDada Press

Choreopoems:

The Jeffers Project, 2013
Reclaiming My Time: An American Griot Project, 2018
Bridge {the Gap}, co-written with Sharia Benn, 2019
RMT 2.0, 2020
Forthcoming: HairStory: Reclaiming Our Crown, 2023

Anthologies:

Come Shining: Poems and Essays On Writing in A Dark Time, Kelson
     Books, 2016
Black Lives Have Always Mattered, 2 Leaf Press ,• 2016
Below the Belt. Poem Sugar Press 2015
The Spirit Speaks Anthology. Poem Sugar Press, 2015
Poetry Ink. Moonstone Press, 2010
Our Words, Our Voices, Writers Worshop
"Natural Woman" Haiku 2021, Moonstone Press, 2021
"#Activism" PPS Anthology: Pennsylvania Poetry Society, 2021
"Essentials" Essential Voices: A Covid19 Anthology, 2021
"A Fuse Blew" Black Lives Have Always Mattered. Ed. Abiodun
     Oyewole. 2Leaf Press, 2017

Journals:

"Gentle Rage" Harrisburg Magazine: Journal Publications, 2021
"Terra Rocks" Cutthroat Journal of the Arts: Cutthroat, 2021
"The Trunk" Like the Rain Fallin' From Heavin, It'll Come: A Tribute to
     Sonia Sanchez: Moonstone Press, 2018.
"Contusion" Cutthroat: A Journal of the Arts. Ed. William Pitt Root.
     Durango: Cutthroat, 2016.
"Those People." The Spirit Speaks Anthology. Ed. Carla Christopher.
     Poem Sugar Press, 2014.

"Only an author who has truly mastered both the instrumentation of words and the instinctual music of the emotions behind them could have written the book Maria James-Thiaw has created."

~ **Carla Christopher**, Poet Laureate of York, PA

TALKING "White"

M A R I A   J A M E S - T H I A W

Available at
amazon

About Maria James-Thiaw

This 2009 Goddard College MFA graduate is the author of four poetry collections and has been published in numerous journals and anthologies including *Black Lives Have Always Mattered, Cutthroat Journal of the Arts, and Essential Voices: A Covid19 Anthology*. Poems from her play, *Reclaiming My Time: An American Griot Project*, won the Art of Protest Award from Penn State University's Center for American Literary Studies in 2018.

Maria James-Thiaw is a recovering educator and the founder of Reclaim Artist Collective, an organization that brings her American Griot Project programming to marginalized communities.

CPSIA information can be obtained
at www.ICGtesting.com
Printed in the USA
BVHW031734160223
658685BV00018B/272